INSIDE
KING TUT'S
TOMB

TOP SECRET

ISAAC KERRY

Lerner Publications ◆ Minneapolis

To Lily and Julia

Lerner Publications Company
An imprint of Lerner Publishing Group, Inc.
241 First Avenue North
Minneapolis, MN 55401 USA

For reading levels and more information, look up this title at www.lernerbooks.com.

Main body text set in Aptifer Sans LT Pro.
Typeface provided by Linotype AG.

Editor: Brianna Kaiser. **Designer:** Athena Currier

Library of Congress Cataloging-in-Publication Data

Names: Kerry, Isaac, author.
Title: Inside King Tut's tomb / Isaac Kerry.
Description: Minneapolis : Lerner Publications, [2023] | Series: Top secret (alternator books) | Includes bibliographical references and index. | Audience: Ages 8–12 | Audience: Grades 4–6 | Summary: "King Tut was an intriguing figure during his life and still was after his mysterious death. Readers will learn the secrets about King Tut, the supposed curse following the discovery of his tomb, and more!"— Provided by publisher.
Identifiers: LCCN 2022015512 (print) | LCCN 2022015513 (ebook) | ISBN 9781728476636 (lib. bdg.) | ISBN 9781728478333 (pbk.) | ISBN 9781728485386 (eb pdf)
Subjects: LCSH: Tutankhamen, King of Egypt—Tomb—Juvenile literature. | Egypt—Antiquities— Juvenile literature.
Classification: LCC DT87.5 .K47 2023 (print) | LCC DT87.5 (ebook) | DDC 932/.014—dc23/eng/20220429

LC record available at https://lccn.loc.gov/2022015512
LC ebook record available at https://lccn.loc.gov/2022015513

Manufactured in the United States of America
1-52244-50684-7/5/2022

TABLE OF CONTENTS

INTRODUCTION

MYSTERIES IN THE SAND

British archaeologist and Egyptologist Howard
Carter looks out over the Egyptian desert. It's November
1922, and time is running out for his excavation in the
Valley of the Kings. If he doesn't find anything soon, he will
run out of money and return to England empty-handed. His
team spreads out in search of the tomb of a lost pharaoh.
Suddenly, Carter hears a shout. A team member has tripped
and fallen. As Carter looks for what caused the fall, he sees
steps leading down into the sand!

Carter and his team quickly remove the sand and dirt.
They are amazed at what they find: the tomb of King

Tutankhamun, known as King Tut! The story of what happened to this young king, as well as what became of the men who discovered his resting place, is full of mysteries.

In 1922 Howard Carter's excavation team found the steps leading down to King Tut's tomb.

CHAPTER I
THE BOY KING'S TOMB

A replica of Tut's burial chamber, including his sarcophagus

Howard Carter with Lord Carnarvon (*left*) around 1922

Carter was interested in Egypt from a young age. In 1891, when he was seventeen, he joined an archaeological expedition to the country. At the time, the British Empire controlled Egypt. Britain had invaded Egypt in 1882, increasing interest in the country. That year the British Egypt Exploration Fund was founded to pay for the excavations of Egyptian sites. Many new archaeological techniques were being developed and practiced.

Carter (*left*) and Carnarvon stand near the wall being removed between the antechamber and burial chamber of Tut's tomb. The antechamber is the biggest room and where other rooms are accessed from.

Carter's work was impressive, and he soon found himself in charge of more advanced expeditions. He began working on excavating burial sites in the Valley of the Kings. Many Egyptian pharaohs were buried there. His interest in the area eventually led him to meet Lord Carnarvon. The wealthy Brit was fascinated by ancient Egypt. In 1915 the two men began a new mission in the Valley of the Kings. Their goal was to find the burial place of King Tut.

A painted wood artifact of Tut on display in 2005

Who Was King Tut?

King Tutankhamun, sometimes spelled Tutankhamen or Tutankhamon, was an Egyptian pharaoh who ruled over three thousand years ago. He became pharaoh when he was about nine. He ruled for ten years before his death around 1324 BCE.

After Tut died, the next Egyptian ruler took control of Tut's monuments and removed him from the list of pharaohs, restricting the memory of him. His tomb was also quite small for a pharaoh. Many historians believe this suggests his death was unexpected. He was buried in the Valley of the Kings.

Over a hundred years after his death, workers constructed huts over the entrance to Tut's tomb. This caused his burial site to be forgotten. Throughout the years, grave robbers broke into the tombs of many pharaohs in the Valley of the Kings. They stole the treasures placed there. Exposing the sites to nature often caused them to be destroyed. Tut's tomb remained unharmed, hidden away beneath the desert.

Harry Burton was a photographer of excavations in the Valley of the Kings. He took many photos of King Tut's tomb.

In 2014 artifacts from Tut's tomb are on display at an exhibition in Slovakia.

CHAPTER 2
LIFE AND DEATH IN EGYPT

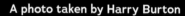
A photo taken by Harry Burton

An inside look at Tut's tomb in Luxor, Egypt, in 2018

After Carter and his team discovered King Tut's tomb on November 4, 1922, they spent several months carefully excavating it. They eventually made their way into the inner burial chamber. There they found over thirty-five hundred ancient Egyptian artifacts. These included jewelry, toys, chariots, and clothing. They also found a stone coffin called a sarcophagus. Inside was the mummified body of Tut.

Carter (*left*) and a colleague examine Tut's coffin in 1926.

He wore a solid gold mask in the shape of his face. The golden face of the dead pharaoh became famous around the world, and people grew fascinated with his story.

Death of a King

No historical record exists of how Tut died. This lack of information has led to several different theories about what could have caused his death. Did he die in an accident? Did he catch some deadly illness? Was he murdered? With modern technology, archaeologists have found some interesting clues to support or disprove these theories.

High-tech scans of Tut's body showed skull damage, leading to the theory he was murdered. He also had a fractured lower leg. So some believed he died after a chariot crash. Images in his tomb show the young king riding chariots, supporting the theory. Such an injury in ancient Egypt could have led to a deadly infection.

Ancient Egyptians had many steps in the mummification process, including wrapping the body in layers of linen. This is Tut's skull in 1926 after the linen wrappings are removed.

Egyptologist Dr. Zahi Hawass (*left*) and a colleague complete a CT scan of Tut's mummy to see inside Tut's body.

SOLVE IT!

///////////////////////////////////

The damage to Tut's skull suggested that he may have been murdered. However, a scan of his body revealed that this damage was caused after his death. Of course, this does not rule out that he could have been the victim of violence. Investigating such an ancient murder would be difficult. But maybe you could discover historical accounts that archaeologists haven't found yet.

The scans also revealed that he suffered from bone deformities—bones a different size or shape than normal. Egyptian royalty often married close relatives. This led to many genetic problems. Scientists think that these problems could have been responsible for Tut's death or made him more likely to get sick. DNA analysis has also shown that Tut had malaria. This disease would have been very dangerous in the ancient past.

As technology advances, scientists will be able to learn more about how this young man died. Until then, his death will remain a mystery.

A cobra is at the top of Tut's death mask.

The Mummy's Curse

On the day Carter's team opened Tut's tomb, a cobra killed Carter's pet canary. Cobras were often associated with Egyptian royalty. The statues of Tut inside his tomb had cobras on their crowns. Newspapers were eager to provide their readers with details of the excavation and ran with this story. They labeled it proof of a curse, suggesting that the snake was a warning from beyond the grave for disturbing Tut's tomb. Carter may have encouraged these stories to keep interested locals away from the dig site.

Many ancient Egyptian royals highly valued cobras, which were a symbol of protection.

THE SARATOGA SUN.

What Killed Carnarvon— Tut-Ankh-Amen's Curse?

LATEST MARKET QUOTATIONS

Many newspapers published stories about Tut's curse. This article about the curse appeared in the *Saratoga* (WY) *Sun* in 1923.

A year later, another tragedy struck. One morning, Carnarvon cut open a mosquito bite while shaving. This tiny cut led to an infection and eventually his death from blood poisoning. The press spread rumors of the curse striking again.

Over the years, other people linked to the excavation died in mysterious and tragic ways. An Egyptian prince who visited the tomb in 1923 was murdered by his wife. The home of one of Carter's friends burned down—twice. Each time some new tragedy happened, people saw it as more evidence of the curse.

SOLVE IT!

///////////////////////////////////

Researching expected life spans is one way you could see if those who worked on Tut's tomb died at unusually young ages. Look up the average lifetime of people in the 1920s to see how long a person was expected to live. Then look up the people who excavated Tut's tomb. How old were they when they died? How do these ages compare to the average life expectancy?

Other people suggest these tragedies were just coincidence. Even Carter never believed in a curse. And he would have been the likely target. He was the first person to open the tomb. While removing the golden burial mask, he even accidentally removed the head from the body! But Carter lived to the age of sixty-four before dying of cancer in 1939. Some people say this proves there was no curse. Others say that the mummy finally took its revenge.

CHAPTER 3
FURTHER SECRETS

Tut's sarcophagus had three coffins inside it. The outer two coffins were made out of wood covered in gold, and the inner coffin was solid gold.

In 2019 an Egyptian archaeologist works on restoring Tut's gilded coffin.

Over a century has passed since Carter opened Tut's tomb and introduced the world to the young pharaoh. Despite years of research and newer technology, the burial site may still have some secrets.

Restorer Olfat Mohamed holds up an artifact from Tut's tomb in 2019.

Mystery Spots

In 2019 a major conservation project of Tut's tomb was completed. Ever since its discovery, the tomb has been a major tourist attraction. Over the years, the stream of visitors introduced many outside elements that threatened the site. The wall paintings and artifacts within the chambers are ancient. Minor changes to their environment such as dust or humidity can damage them.

Tut's tomb is covered in wall paintings.

Workers installed protective equipment to keep visitors a safe distance from the tomb's contents. They also installed a ventilation system to remove particles and regulate the air.

While cleaning the wall paintings in the tomb, workers made a strange discovery. Small brown spots were all over the walls. Photos of Carter's excavation showed that the spots were present during the discovery of the tomb. The spots have merged with the paint of the walls. Removing the spots would damage the ancient artwork.

A wall painting from Tut's tomb in 2019

DECLASSIFIED

The Egyptian queen Nefertiti was one of the wives of King Tut's father, King Akhenaten. After Akhenaten died around 1336 BCE, Nefertiti may have ruled over Egypt as pharaoh until Tut's reign began. But Nefertiti disappeared from historical records sometime during Akhenaten's reign, so we don't know for sure.

Nefertiti's resting place has not been found. Her daughter Ankhesenamun married Tut, so some scholars believe Nefertiti's tomb is near his. The most recent survey of the area found what appears to be a space near Tut's tomb. It is the same distance belowground and runs parallel to Tut's chambers. Unrelated tombs are not usually parallel. More research might determine if Nefertiti's tomb is near Tut's. Doing any physical digging would be extremely difficult due to the threat of damaging Tut's tomb.

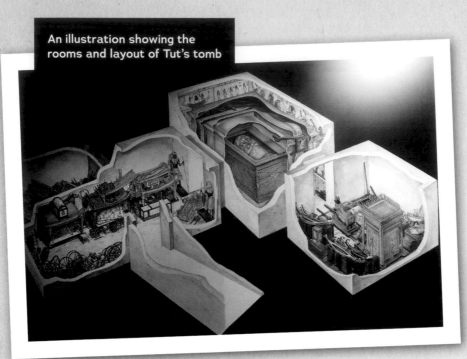

An illustration showing the rooms and layout of Tut's tomb

Secrets in the Walls

One of the most intriguing modern mysteries of the tomb is the potential for secret chambers hidden in its walls. Some Egyptologists have suspected that certain cracks in the tomb's walls could be hidden doorways. Many scientists have tried to test this theory. They used different kinds of radar to examine the walls and search for openings. Some of these studies suggested there are hidden chambers, while others seemed to disprove this. Given the many mysteries surrounding King Tut's tomb, it's fitting that modern science cannot yet solve all of them.

Timeline

ca. 1332 BCE: King Tutankhamun becomes pharaoh.

ca. 1324 BCE: He rules until his death.

1882: The British Empire invades Egypt.

The British Egypt Exploration Fund was founded to pay for excavations in Egypt.

1915: Lord Carnarvon gains the rights to explore the Valley of the Kings. He hires Howard Carter to lead his expeditions.

1922: On November 4, Carter and his team find the staircase of Tut's tomb.

On November 26, they enter the tomb's chambers and find the mummy of Tut and ancient artifacts.

1923: Carnarvon dies of blood poisoning on April 5 in Cairo, Egypt.

1939: Carter dies on March 2 from cancer.

2019: A ten-year restoration project of Tut's tomb is completed.

Glossary

archaeologist: a scientist who studies human history and culture by exploring ancient sites and researching artifacts

associate: to connect to something

conservation: the practice of keeping and protecting ancient locations and artifacts

Egyptologist: someone who studies the history and civilization of ancient Egypt

excavate: to remove earth and stone at buried ancient sites

expedition: a journey taken for a reason, such as to excavate Egypt

mummy: a dead body from ancient Egypt preserved with chemicals and wrapped in cloth

pharaoh: the name given to the kings and queens of ancient Egypt

theory: an explanation for why something happened

tomb: a large structure used to bury the dead

Learn More

Archaeology: Clues from the Past
https://www.amnh.org/explore/ology/archaeology

Kenney, Karen Latchana. *Mysteries of the Egyptian Pyramids*.
Minneapolis: Lerner Publications, 2018.

Mummy Mystery: King Tut
https://kids.nationalgeographic.com/history/article/king-tut

Oachs, Emily Rose. *King Tut's Tomb*. Minneapolis: Bellwether
Media, 2020.

O'Neill, Sean. *50 Things You Didn't Know about Ancient Egypt*.
South Egremont, MA: Red Chair, 2020.

Peterson, Megan Cooley. *King Tut: Is His Tomb Really Cursed?*
Mankato, MN: Black Rabbit Books, 2019.

Tutankhamun Facts for Kids
https://kids.kiddle.co/Tutankhamun

Understanding Ancient Egypt
https://www.historyforkids.net/ancient-egypt.html

Index

Photo Acknowledgments

Image credits: Heidelberg University Library, pp. 5, 10, 12; Gary Warnimont/ Alamy Stock Photo, p. 6; David Cole/Alamy Stock Photo, p. 7; Harry Burton/ Wikimedia Commons (PD) p. 8; REUTERS/Fred Prouser/Alamy Stock Photo, p. 9; Jaroslav Moravcik/Shutterstock, p. 11; Nick Brundle Photography/Shutterstock, p. 13; Pictorial Press Ltd/Alamy Stock Photo, p. 14; Wellcome Collection, p. 15; Danita Delimont/Alamy Stock Photo, p. 16; AP Photo/Amr Nabil, p. 18; Hemis/Alamy Stock Photo, p. 19; The Saratoga Sun/Library of Congress, p. 20; imageBROKER/Alamy Stock Photo, p. 22; Hassan Mohamed/dpa/Alamy Live News, p. 23; AP Photo/Matt Dunham, p. 24; Westmorland Images/Getty Images, p. 25; Ahmed Gomaa/Xinhua/Alamy Live News, p. 26; Kevin E. Schmidt/Quad-City Times/ZUMA Wire/Alamy Live News, p. 28.

Design elements: fotograzia/Getty Images; Ivan Gromov/Unsplash; Marjan Blan/ Unsplash; Reddavebatcave/Shutterstock; AVS-Images/Shutterstock.

Cover: Anton Belot/Shutterstock.